OLD FORT SNELLING

Instruction Book for Fife

With Music of Early America

By Donald E. Mattson and Louis D. Walz

MINNESOTA HISTORICAL SOCIETY PRESS □ ST. PAUL

International Standard Book Number: 0-87351-090-9
Printed in Canada

10 9 8 7 6

◉ The paper used in this publication meets the minimum requirements of the American National Standard for Information Sciences—Permanence for Printed Library Materials, ANSI Z39.48-1984.

Library of Congress Cataloging in Publication Data:
Mattson, Donald E   1929-
   Old Fort Snelling instruction book for fife, with
music of early America.

   (Minnesota historic sites pamphlet series, no. 11)
(Publications of the Minnesota Historical Society)
   Bibliography: p.
   1. Fife—Methods. I. Walz, Louis D., 1897-
joint author. II. Title. III. Series. IV. Series:
Minnesota Historical Society. Publications.
MT356.M27   788'.51'0712   74-7298

The Company of Military Historians through its Review Board takes pleasure in endorsing this book as an accurate and useful reference work in military history.

Dedicated to the field musicians of the Fifth United States Infantry, Fort Snelling, 1819-1828, the first professional American musical group in what is now the state of Minnesota

ACKNOWLEDGMENTS

The authors wish to thank Dr. Edgar M. Turrentine, professor of music, University of Minnesota, for information and guidance; Mr. William Kugler, founder of the Kugler Museum of Musical Instruments, St. Paul, for his encouragement and for permission to use music from an 1805 manuscript in his collection; and the members of the Company of Military Historians Review Board -- George P. Carroll, Edward Olsen, and William F. Gallagher -- for their advice and suggestions.

We are also indebted for historical material and technical assistance to: Colonel William H. Schempe, director, United States Military Academy Band, West Point; Chief Warrant Officer Victor F. Owens, Old Guard Fife and Drum Corps, Third Infantry, United States Army; Mr. Theodore Kurtz, fife manufacturer; and Robert C. Price, principal fifer, Old Fort Snelling Fife and Drum Corps.

Many people helped make this publication possible, and to all of them we express our sincere thanks. We are particularly grateful to Mr. John Grossman and other members of the Minnesota Historical Society's Historic Fort Snelling restoration staff, whose interest in fife and drum music inspired the development of this volume, and to the members of the society's publications department -- Mrs. June D. Holmquist, Miss Carolyn Gilman, Alan Ominsky, and Bruce M. White -- for helpful suggestions and for seeing the volume through the press. The illustrations are the work of Dale H. Peterson, and the music copy was prepared by Leonard Borlaug and Bruce M. White.

I would also like to express my personal appreciation to my wife, Wanoma, for her patience and assistance during the preparation of this work.

Donald E. Mattson

ABOUT THE AUTHORS

LIEUTENANT COLONEL DONALD E. MATTSON, United States Army, is an alumnus of Vandercook College of Music in Chicago and Minnesota Metropolitan State College in St. Paul. In addition to his regular military duties, he is director of the Old Fort Snelling Fife and Drum Corps and consultant to the Minnesota Historical Society's Fort Snelling restoration. His previous experience includes service as band master of the Seventh Infantry Division Band, drum major and solo trumpet of the Thirty-third Infantry Division Band, and solo trumpet in the Ninth Battalion Band, United States Marine Reserve. His interest in the fife developed from a study of Old Fort Snelling's musical groups which he made for the Minnesota Historical Society. Colonel Mattson became acquainted with Captain Walz, his former teacher and the coauthor of this book, as a student and member of the Lakeview High School Band of Chicago in the 1940s.

CAPTAIN LOUIS D. WALZ, an alumnus of Vandercook College of Music and a former member of the Illinois National Guard, provided the basic material for the fife instruction method used in this book. Born in Winona, Minnesota, in 1897, Captain Walz's musical experience stretches back to provide continuity with the musicians of the Civil War, for he learned to play the fife as a boy of nine and participated as a fifer in many encampments of the Grand Army of the Republic. Later he played solo cornet in mounted and marching bands in World War I, taught and directed the Continental Bank Post of the American Legion Fife and Drum Corps in Chicago, and was an instructor of instrumental music at the American Conservatory of Music in Chicago in the 1930s. From 1928 until his retirement in 1961, Captain Walz was a teacher and band director in Lakeview High School.

CONTENTS

ILLUSTRATIONS

MUSIC AT OLD FORT SNELLING

THE FIRST professional musicians in what is now Minnesota were the fifers and drummers of the Fifth United States Infantry Regiment. The Fifth Infantry, commanded by Lieutenant Colonel Henry Leavenworth, was ordered to the junction of the Minnesota and Mississippi rivers in 1819 to build a fort in order to break the hold of British fur traders on the Indians of the area. Colonel Josiah Snelling assumed command shortly thereafter; he selected the fort site and supervised its construction. The fort was named in his honor after an inspection tour in 1824.

Field music in this period was provided by fifes and drums, and musicians were among the advance party of the Fifth Infantry regiment which traveled up the Mississippi River to the site of the new fort in August, 1819. The troops were apparently in a carefree mood, for it is reported that they sang as they traveled such old favorites as "Yankee Doodle" and "The Girl I Left Behind Me" -- tunes which became a part of Fort Snelling's history.

The muster rolls of the Fifth Infantry show that twelve to fourteen musicians were usually stationed at Fort Snelling. A fifer and drummer were authorized for each company in a regiment. In addition to the six fifers and six drummers for the six companies at the fort, the senior principal musician (or drum major) and the junior principal musician (or fife major) were posted at Fort Snelling because it was the regimental headquarters. The drum major led the massed fifers and drummers, and the fife major marched to the right of the front rank of fifers. One bugler is shown on the rolls as a musician for Light Infantry Company B. Because the bugle is audible for greater distances, it was his duty to sound the field maneuver signals for that group.

Dr. Nathan S. Jarvis, who served as army surgeon at Fort Snelling from 1833 to 1836, described the role of music at this remote outpost. "The uniformity of garrison life is like clock work," he wrote. "1st at day light the reveillie beats for about 15 minutes all the drums & fifes marching the whole circuit of the barracks to awaken the whole, who must all turn out except [the] sick on parade . . . The next call beats at 20 minutes before 7 o'clock which is the sick call . . . At 7 o'clock is breakfast call . . . parades & drilling fill up the interval of the day between dinner and supper. Retreat beats at sun down which is here as late as 8 o'clock. . . . Tat[t]oo is at 9 o'clock when our band of which we have a very good one plays a number of favourite tunes, and all return to their beds."

A tune entitled "Peas Upon a Trencher" was used at Fort Snelling for both breakfast and supper calls. Dinner call was "Roast Beef," borrowed from the English "Roast Beef of Merry Old England." (Both tunes are included in this booklet.) Other posts used various tunes. The Sixth Infantry at Fort Atkinson in Kansas, for example, played "Molly Put the Kettle On" as a breakfast call.

Fifes and drums were used in garrison and in battle. "Three Camps" or "Three Points of War" was played at reveille, and tattoo for bedtime. In battle these instruments sounded the signals for "march," "advance by the double step," "cease firing," "retreat," and many other calls. (See page 92, below). Airs and popular tunes of the day were played to lift the spirits of the troops and provide music for military ceremonies. "Yankee Doodle" and "Hail Columbia" were favorites; "The Star-Spangled Banner" was also played, but it was not as popular as the others. When troops were dispatched from Fort Snelling on a mission, it was customary for the fifes and drums to play "The Girl I Left Behind Me." For formal guard mount and dress parade, the musicians trooped the line playing a tune called "Three Cheers," which is said to have originated during the crusades. Two tempos were used during a review. The troops first passed marching in common time of 90 beats to the minute and then in quick time of 120 beats to the minute. Most soldiers preferred to march in quick time rather than the slower, more difficult common time.

Although subject to the hardships of the frontier, Fort Snelling was the scene of an active social life, and the musicians were often called upon to play at officers' dances and parties as well as at parades and the daily flag-raising ceremony. All too frequently the band performed a sadder duty, playing a dirge (probably "Roslin Castle" or "Dead March in Saul") at a soldier's funeral.

At least one Fifth Infantry musician later played a prominent role in Minnesota's development. He was Joseph R. Brown, who enlisted as a private in 1820 and served as a fifer and drummer at Fort Snelling. After he was discharged from the army as a sergeant in 1828, Brown chose to remain in Minnesota, becoming a fur trader, Indian agent to the Dakota (Sioux), and later a major in charge of volunteers at the battle of Birch Coulee during the Dakota War of 1862.

In the 1840s and 1850s the bands of the Fifth, Sixth, and Tenth Infantry regiments enlivened many a pioneer ball in the growing nearby frontier villages of St. Anthony, St. Paul, and Stillwater. When the frontier moved farther west, Fort Snelling was briefly closed, but the flag that had been lowered in silence in 1858 was raised again to the drums and fifes of the First Minnesota Volunteer Regiment in 1861 as the fort was reopened to serve as a recruiting and draft rendezvous in the Civil War. Musicians and their units were organized and trained at the old fort before embarking for the South to the strains of "The Girl I Left Behind Me." The Second Minnesota Volunteer Regiment won renown for its fife, drum, and bugle band during this conflict.

Fort Snelling ended its 126-year career as an active army post with the sounding of a final "retreat" by drums and bugles on October 15, 1946. Today martial music resounds once more within the rebuilt stone walls of the old fort. The very same drum signals and fife tunes which called the garrison to work and parade in the 1820s are again heard as the Fort Snelling restoration, financed by the state of Minnesota and administered by the Minnesota Historical Society, re-creates frontier life at the junction of the Minnesota and Mississippi rivers. The 20th century Fife and Drum Corps of Old Fort Snelling is a voluntary association dedicated to the authentic preservation and performance of the musical heritage of the fifers and drummers of the Fifth Infantry. The method of instruction outlined in the pages that follow was developed and has been used successfully with this group.

HISTORY OF THE FIFE

THIS BOOK offers an instruction method for the Bb fife as well as selected tunes from the 1750s until shortly after the Civil War, the period of the fife's greatest popularity in the United States. Because of the prominent role of fifes and long drums during the Revolutionary War and the early years of the republic, these instruments have become traditional symbols of the young nation and of its heritage.

The forerunner of the fife is an instrument known as the cross flute or transverse flute. Recorded history reveals references to cross flutes in China as early as the 9th century B.C. By the 10th and 11th centuries A.D. they had made their way via Byzantium to Europe, where they became especially prominent in the folk music of many areas east of the Rhine River. With the adoption of the cross flute by German and Swiss peasants, the names Zwerchpfeiffen (cross pipe) and Schweitzerpfeiffen (Swiss fife) appeared, marking the beginning of the term "fife." From Switzerland and Germany the instrument spread rapidly throughout Europe during the later Middle Ages.

The fife has been associated with military music at least since the early 1500s when Swiss troops used both fifes and drums for command and control in battle. A century later Michael Praetorius described the Swiss fife as being two feet long and having a range from G^1 (of the first octave) to C^3 (of the third octave) or $C\#^1$ to $A\#^2$. In 1534 the use of the fife was prescribed by regulation for French troops -- two fifes and two drums for each company of a thousand men -- and during the same period fifers were brought to England for the king's band. By 1539 the English citizenry played fifes and drums at Christmas festivities, and by the 1550s and 1560s fifes and drums were being used on the English stage and in the British army.

The fife was banished from the British army during the reign of James II (1685-88). Oliver Cromwell referred to it as a profane instrument, and Shakespeare wrote of its "vile squealing" and "ear-piercing" qualities in "The Merchant of Venice" and in "Othello." Although the fife fell into disuse by the British, it persisted among the Germans and French, and it was reintroduced to the British Foot Guards by a young Hanoverian about 1745.

Because it was one of the best instruments to keep soldiers marching in step, the fife soon spread to other regiments of the British army who brought it to America. As early as 1756 Benjamin Franklin, then a militia colonel in Philadelphia, passed his regiment in review with hautboys and fifes in the ranks. In Boston in 1764 "fife tutors" (instruction books) as well as fifes were advertised for sale, and four years later an account relates that British troops landed and marched to the Boston Common with colors flying, drums beating, and fifes playing. Interestingly enough, "Yankee Doodle" was often played by the British as well as by the Americans. It was not uncommon for British military bands to play the tune, sometimes to ridicule the colonists.

The fife begins to assume its symbolic role in American history with the Boston Tea Party on the night of December 16, 1773. As the participants returned from that historic event, they marched to the spirited sounds of the fife. The minutemen at Lexington and Concord in April, 1775, also used fifes and drums. The company fifer and drummer sounded signals and played "The White Cockade" at Concord Bridge. At Bunker Hill in 1775 colonial fifers and drummers played "Yankee Doodle" for the first time in battle.

During the Revolutionary War, each colony provided militia troops who normally had one or two fifers and drummers for each company, and

as early as July, 1775, George Washington, the newly appointed commander in chief, was issuing orders concerning the instruction of fifers and drummers in the Continental Army, which was plagued by a shortage of instruments. The Continental Congress authorized fifes and drums for the Continental Army.

Fifes of the American colonial period were cruder in workmanship and finish than those of a later date. They were for the most part imported from Europe, primarily from England, or made domestically. The blow holes and finger holes were burned instead of drilled in some of the domestic fifes. American instrument makers were not numerous; many made flutes but very few specifically listed fifes. During the Revolutionary War it is known that Major Jonathan Gostelow set up a drum factory and delivered 54 drums and 163 fifes to the Continental Army on August 23, 1780.

The instrument used in most early American fife and drum corps was a B♭ fife about 17 inches long, although some British military fifes about 15 inches long with a pitch of C were also used. Because of lack of standardization and differences in the quality of craftsmanship, fifes were produced in such varying keys and pitches that George Washington ordered that they be sorted according to pitch so the musicians in the Continental Army could play together in tune.

Music regulated the soldier's life in that army. A series of beats and signals performed by fifes and drums governed the soldier's every move, as they did at such later frontier posts as Fort Snelling. They told him when to get up, when to eat, and when to go to bed, and they also directed his movements in battle or in military ceremonies.

Twenty-one beats and signals for the Continental Army were standardized and adapted by Washington's talented helper the Prussian-born Baron Friedrich Von Steuben. Von Steuben's regulations listed nine beats: The General, The Assembly, The March, The Reveille, The Troop, The Retreat, The Tattoo, To Arms, and The Parley.

They also prescribed the following twelve signals: Adjutant's Call, First Sergeant's Call, Noncommissioned Officers' Call, Go for Wood, Go for Water, Go for Provisions, Front Halt, Front Advance Quicker, Front March Slower, Drummers Call, Fatigue Call, and Church Call.

Over the years melodies changed and some beats and signals were modified or added while others were dropped. In 1836 when Fort Snelling was in its heyday, the War Department's regulations listed twenty-two signals and beats.

The drum was the primary instrument for conveying signals and commands. Fife music was added to the beats, however, for a combined musical company. Music for some of these may be found on pages 92-105, below.

These beats and signals were augmented by the playing of popular tunes on long marches or festive camp occasions. The fifes were accompanied by the beating of the drum, and we find such tunes as "Chester," "Washington's March," "Old Continental March," and "On the Road to Boston" being played during the Revolutionary War.

Music also played a role in the surrender of the British at Yorktown, Virginia, in October, 1781, which virtually marked the end of the Revolutionary War. At the surrender ceremony, the allied French and American troops were lined up in two groups facing each other. As the surrendering British marched between them, their band is said to have played in a mournful manner "The World Turned Upside Down" or "Down, Down, Derry Down." One account relates that as the British troopers passed rank by rank every English soldier turned his eyes to the French as if to blot out the Americans. Lafayette noticed this and "revenged himself in a very pleasant manner" by ordering the American light infantry musicians to strike up "Yankee Doodle."

With the end of the Revolutionary War, the Continental Army was disbanded in 1784. When the fifers and drummers were mustered out, they were allowed to keep their instruments, which retained their popularity in the civilian life of the country and in the soon-to-be-formed United States Army.

Over the years they continued to play a military role as the frontiers of the United States rolled westward and the nation engaged in various conflicts. When the United States Marine Corps was established by law in 1798, 32 drums and fifes were authorized. In 1800 a Philadelphia newspaper reported that the fifes and drums of the original Marine band played "Yankee Doo-dle," "On the Road to Boston," "Roslin Castle," and "Washington's March" -- tunes included in this book. Until about 1800 the Marine band consisted solely of fifes and drums. Even after other instruments were added, the Marines used fifes until about 1875, when the farther-carry-ing bugle replaced the fife for field calls.

The importance of the instruments is indi-cated by the fact that a school for fifers and drummers of the United States Army was estab-lished at Fort Columbus on Governor's Island, New York, in 1809. Its purpose was to stand-ardize fifing and drumming throughout the army, and it remained in operation until the time of the Civil War.

The school was influential in a number of ways. About 1841 or 1842 a drum major named Crosby who was associated with the school re-quested local manufacturers to deliver a lower-pitched fife than the English military B♭ mod-el (which actually had a pitch of C). The re-sult of this request was the development of the B♭ Crosby fife with a much better tone. Crosby fifes were made by Firth, Hall and Pond (1848-65) of New York and by Walter Crosby, a Boston manufacturer. During the Civil War George and Frederick Cloos were the largest suppliers of B♭ fifes in the United States, and they contin-ued to make instruments well into the 20th century.

Another instructor in the Governor's Island school was George B. Bruce, who in 1862 collabo-rated with Daniel D. Emmett in the publication of The Drummer's and Fifer's Guide. Emmett, who is better known as a famous minstrel and the com-poser of "Dixie," had served a short stint in the United States Army in 1834-35, where he be-came the principal fifer of the Sixth United States Infantry at Jefferson Barracks, Missouri. Although it was written in 1859, "Dixie," of course, later came to be associated with the Con-federate Army of the Civil War.

About 1861, when the Civil War broke out, brass bands became very popular in the United States. After the Civil War, fifes and drums continued to be used as field music until chang-ing battle tactics and equipment required the adoption of the bugle in 1875. Army regulations, however, still permitted the use of the fife in place of the bugle as an optional item for foot troops as late as 1917. The general popularity and use of the fife declined after it was dropped by the army, and brass bands gained as-cendancy. Field music was abolished by the army shortly before World War II when such modern com-munication methods as radio and telephone re-moved the need for musical signals in battle. After that brass bands became traditional for ceremonial purposes.

The veterans of the Civil War had many a lo-cal Grand Army of the Republic fife and drum corps long after the close of that conflict, but time gradually depleted their ranks. Over the years an interest in fifes and long drums persisted in the northeastern part of the United States, especially in New York and Connecticut, and kept alive this aspect of American music for later generations.

CHARACTERISTICS AND CARE OF THE FIFE

THE FIFE is a wind instrument, a member of the cross (or transverse) flute family, so called because air is blown across a blow hole while the instrument is held horizontal to the ground. The fife is characterized by a smaller diameter of the cylindrical bore than the flute, and it is this feature which gives the instrument a shrill or piercing tone on higher notes. The flute's larger bore allows the lower octaves to be played more easily. Fifes have varied in pitch and in size, ranging from 13 inches to 2 feet. They normally have six finger holes.

The fife is an inexpensive instrument which enables many students to begin musical training at an early age. The student of the fife will also find it of value in learning to play other instruments.

Wooden fifes are generally made of granadilla, cocobolo, ebony, or boxwood. They may chip or crack if they are not cared for properly and protected from cold. A new wooden fife should be oiled once or twice a week for two months, then once a month for eight months, and two or three times a year thereafter.

Dry the fife after each use by swabbing with a soft cloth. Then swab it inside and wipe the outside with a light coat of vegetable oil -- olive oil, linseed oil, or woodwind oil. It was a common practice for military fifers to use a chicken feather to spread the oil within the bore of the fife. From time to time they also loaded the fife with oil and allowed it to stand in the instrument overnight.

Fifes made of metal or plastic require only occasional cleaning for hygienic reasons, but unless they are well made, they do not usually have the good tonal quality found in standard wooden fifes.

The pitch of a fife can be adjusted by pushing the cork closer to or away from the blow hole. Pitch can also be affected while playing by turning the blow hole in or away from the lower lip. The player should become familiar with the subtleties of his fife as each instrument has minor but characteristic differences.

The music for the fife is written in the treble clef from D, the first space below the staff, to B, the second space above the staff (see illustration below). Fife music has traditionally been written in this manner, although the actual sound of the notes is one octave higher than they appear on the staff. The fife has the capability to sound three full octaves, the low octave, the middle octave, and the high octave. The higher notes give a piercing sound that can be heard for a great distance. In these pages the lower sounds (or octave) will be dispensed with because they are too low to be heard above the drums.

The overall length of the fife and the size of its bore normally determine the instrument's pitch. Present-day fifes are available in B♭, C, and D. The most commonly used is the B♭ fife. The C and D fifes are higher in pitch and difficult to play in the upper register.

Transposition of fife music can be accomplished in a concert situation to achieve consonance when playing with other instruments. The B♭ fife playing B♭ trumpet music must transpose the music up one full tone. The C fife would transpose the same music down a tone and the D fife would transpose down two tones. To blend the B♭ fife with the G bugle, transpose the fife down one-half tone and to blend it with the F bugle, transpose the music down one and one-half tones.

NORMAL RANGE AND MANNER OF WRITING MUSIC FOR FIFE

RUDIMENTS OF MUSIC

These rudiments of music must be understood before fife instruction is taken up:

The staff consists of five lines and four spaces. Those above and below the staff are called ledger lines.

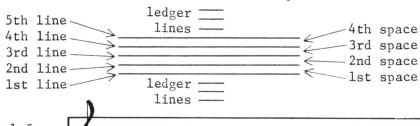

5th line
4th line
3rd line
2nd line
1st line

ledger lines

4th space
3rd space
2nd space
1st space

ledger lines

Fife music is written in the G or treble clef.

Names of the notes in the treble clef are:

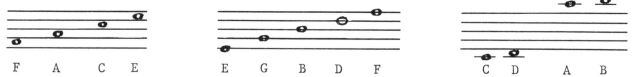

F   A   C   E   E   G   B   D   F   C   D   A   B

Below are some time signatures. The upper figure indicates the number of beats in a measure; the lower figure, which kind of note receives one beat: half (2), quarter (4), or eighth (8).

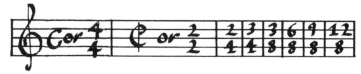

Music is divided into equal parts by lines drawn through the staff;   these are
called bars. The space between two bars is called a measure:

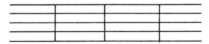

A double bar consists of two lines in the staff and signifies the end of a strain:

Two dots before a double bar indicate that the strain which precedes it should be repeated.
The beginning of the section to be repeated is indicated by two dots after a double bar.

Note values in common or 4/4 time and corresponding rests:

A rest is a mark of silence that instructs the player to stop playing and rest for the
length of time called for by the value of the rest. The bottom line indicates rests
having the same time value as the notes above.

DOTTED NOTES

A dot after a note increases its value by one-half. Two dots increase the note's value by three-fourths.

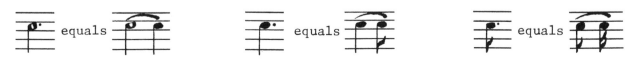

KEY SIGNATURES

A sharp # placed before a note raises it a half tone.

A flat ♭ placed before a note lowers it a half tone.

A double sharp ## raises the note one whole tone.

A double flat ♭♭ lowers the note a whole tone.

A natural ♮ placed before a note restores the note to its original sound.

Keys G, D, and A major will be used in the following lessons. An accomplished fifer can play in other keys, but these three should be mastered before others are attempted.

The key signature is indicated immediately following the clef sign. The sharp on the top line of G major is on the F line of the staff. Therefore all corresponding F notes will be played sharp. The same principle applies to other keys. In D major both the F and C are sharp. For the key of A major, the F, C, and G are sharp.

The term "key" indicates the dominant note of a tune or exercise. In the key of G major, G will be the dominant note; in D major, D will be dominant, etc.

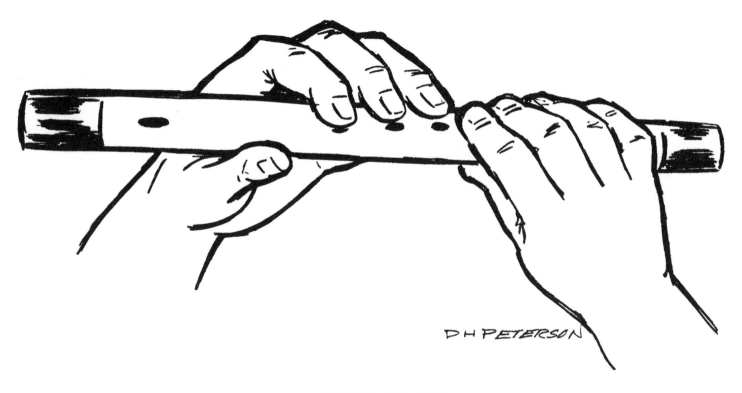

HOLDING THE FIFE

LESSON 1

TONE

An accomplished fifer is recognized by his ability to produce good tonal quality, although fingering technique and proficiency in reading music cannot be disregarded.

To obtain a tone, the blow hole of the fife is placed just below the bottom of the lower lip. To start a tone, a steady stream of air is directed across the blow hole. The intensity of the air determines whether the note will be played high or low (octave).

Each tone is started by the tongue striking the biting edge of the upper teeth as though you were pronouncing the syllable "Ta." This articulation is called single tonguing, and it is used to start a tone or to separate a tone. Practice this technique slowly until you can sound the note easily.

HOLDING THE FIFE

The fife is held horizontal to the ground and pointing toward the right. (See illustration on page 14.) Place the blow hole at the bottom of your lower lip and hold the fife in the left hand resting against the root of the index finger. The thumb is placed under or near the first hole. The bottom pad of the index finger covers the first hole. The second and third fingers cover the second and third holes.

The right hand is placed so the palm is facing downward. Place the thumb under the third or fourth hole. The first, second, and third fingers of the right hand cover the fourth, fifth, and sixth holes. Rest the little finger on the top far right portion of the fife. Let the pads of your fingers fall naturally to cover the holes. When they are not covering the holes, keep the fingers approximately one-half inch above the holes.

Refer constantly to the fingering chart inside the back cover, which illustrates fingering combinations for the various notes of the scale. From the beginning, fingering should be memorized. Memorization is necessary because fifers do not carry music when performing. Remember, try to execute fingering combinations in a free and easy manner.

The first four lines of music on the next page

are composed of whole notes which receive four beats each. Lines 5 and 6 contain half notes which receive two beats each. The clef, time signature, and key are also indicated at the beginning of the line. One must memorize the fingering of the notes in each lesson in order to be an able fifer.

Whole notes in 4/4 time receive 4 beats each.
(Refer to fingering chart; memorize fingering of each note.)

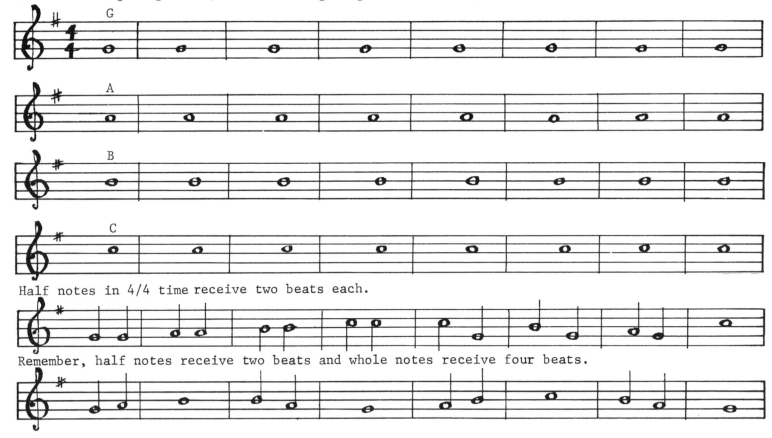

Half notes in 4/4 time receive two beats each.

Remember, half notes receive two beats and whole notes receive four beats.

LESSON 2

THIS LESSON introduces additional notes (tones), rests, the slur, and the repeat sign.

The first three lines are devoted to the whole note. Line 2 introduces the half rest (a bar resting on the third line). Playing long tones builds the fifer's "lip" or embouchure. Embouchure is the application and co-ordination of the muscles of the lips and tongue in playing an instrument. Embouchure must be developed by the player, and development is achieved by practice. Memorize the new notes.

Line 4 introduces the quarter note. Line 5 introduces both octaves of D and a quarter rest as well as a dotted half note in the final measure. A dot after the note increases its value by one-half. Practice both octaves until you can play them with confidence.

Line 6 combines all the types of notes in this lesson, repeats the quarter rest, and introduces the slur. A slur is shown by a curved line connecting two or more notes. It is played without tonguing or stopping the air current. The two dots in the last measure mean that the strain is to be repeated or played again.

ADDITIONAL NOTES AND HALF RESTS

(Play notes slowly to develop tone and embouchure)

High and low D are played with the same fingering.
(To reach higher notes the air stream must be more intense.)

Quarter notes in 4/4 time receive one beat.

The dotted half note in the last measure below receives 3 beats.

Observe the quarter rest in measure 4 below and the last measure above.

Slur   Repeat

LESSON 3

THIS LESSON introduces a complete scale in the key of D. Play each note for four beats to improve tone and range. Practice slowly and memorize the fingering. The C and F are now sharp. Refer to the fingering chart when necessary. Use the models at bottom of page 21 and apply to each note of the D scale. Practice frequently to develop tonguing and familiarity with various notes of the scale.

Line 2 on the following page is an interval exercise and introduces a high E and a low C#. Play low C# with the same fingering as middle C#.

Line 3 introduces eighth notes and rests in the key of G major. The arrows indicate the down and up beat time values.

Line 4 introduces high F# and G. For correct fingering refer to the fingering chart.

Lines 5 and 6 include a simple melody in the key of G major. Notice the key signature, the repeated strain, and the natural C.

TONGUING MODELS

The models on page 21 are designed to develop the player's ability to tongue notes rapidly. The models are arranged in the simple rhythm patterns normally encountered in fife music.

To understand how these exercises can help you, take the first model which is composed of eight eighth notes in 4/4 time (meaning that each note receives one-half beat) and play the first note of the D major scale on the opposite page. Now apply the same model to the second note of the scale, which is E. And the third note, which if F, and so on through all the notes, until you have played the entire scale both up and down several times.

After you have mastered the first model, go on to the second. It is composed of eight sixteenth notes in two-four (2/4) time (meaning two beats per measure). Four sixteenth notes receive a total of one beat. Apply this model to the first note of the D major scale, then to the second note, and so on until you can play the entire scale both up and down.

The remaining tonguing models can be similarly applied to the D major scale. They are also useful for acquiring proficiency in the other scales in Lessons 4 and 5 below.

Once the player has mastered single tonguing (see Lesson 1), he may attempt double and triple

tonguing using these models (see Lesson 13). However, the student is cautioned that each lesson should be mastered before attempting the next one.

D MAJOR SCALE

Practice the scale slowly and gradually increase tempo and play as half, quarter, and eighth notes.

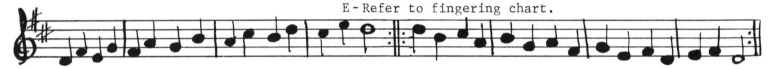

After mastering the above scale, apply the models on the opposite page to each note above.

E - Refer to fingering chart.

EIGHTH NOTES AND EIGHTH RESTS

(Exercise in G Major, C is now ♮.)

(Eighth notes receive one half beat; arrows indicate down and up beats)

MELODY IN 2/4 TIME

(Play two beats to a measure)

TONGUING MODELS

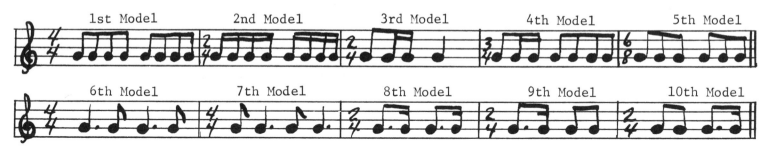

LESSON 4

THIS LESSON includes a complete scale in the key of G. Play each note slowly for four beats to improve tone and range. Practice slowly and memorize the fingering. Apply the models in Lesson 3 to each note of the G major scale. Practice frequently to develop tonguing and familiarity with the various notes of the scale.

Line 2 introduces 3/4 (three-four) time. Look at the time signature listed in the rudiments of music on page 11. Three-four time is a triple rhythm and is usually played three beats to a measure for slow songs and one beat to a measure for fast tunes.

The last portion of this lesson is devoted to the hymn "America" and includes the slur and the dotted eighth note. The melody, which is that of the British national anthem "God Save the King," was played in early America under such titles as "God Save Great Washington" (1796) and "God Save America" (1789). The words to "America" were written in 1831 by Samuel Francis Smith, a young New England clergyman, under the title "My Country 'tis of Thee," a poem he set to the music of "God Save the King" which he found in a German songbook.

G MAJOR SCALE (Notice the F is #)

Practice the scale slowly. Gradually increase the tempo and play as half, quarter, and eighth notes. (After mastering the scale apply the models in Lesson 3 to each note.)

Notice the time signature change. Notes have the same value as in 2/4 or 4/4 time.

DOTTED QUARTER NOTES

Dotted quarter notes may seem difficult but careful study will make this example playable.

Eighth notes marked with > (Accent) are played louder than those marked P (Soft).

AMERICA

LESSON 5

LINE 1 introduces a complete scale in the key of A. Play each note for four beats to improve tone and range. Practice slowly and memorize the fingering for high G♯ and A. Apply the models of Lesson 3 to this scale. Practice frequently to develop tonguing and familiarity with the notes of the scale.

Line 2 is an excellent exercise for intervals. In this line we have a high and low G♯ and a high B. B is as high as one will normally play. Refer to the fingering chart and observe repeat signs.

Lines 3 and 4 are an exercise in 2/4 time designed to develop familiarity with both the eighth note and the sixteenth note. Notice the arrows for the down and up beats and the rhythm examples which are included for a better understanding of this rhythm figure. This exercise is played two beats per measure. Give the dotted eighth note nearly an entire beat and play the sixteenth note just before the next beat.

Lines 5 and 6 introduce a 2/4 melody entitled "Wearing of the Green," which was also known as "The Rising of the Moon." In 1838 this old tune, whose origins are the subject of considerable dispute, was given new words and a new title, "Benny Havens, Oh!," in honor of Benny Havens, who kept a tavern near West Point frequented by Edgar Allan Poe and generations of cadets from the 1830s to the 1870s. Subsequent West Point classes added more verses, and the song was popular with troops in the Civil War.

Observe the dotted eighth and sixteenth notes, as well as the D.C. at the end of the last line. The latter indicates that the first strain is to be repeated. The figure ⌢ (meaning *fine* or finish) indicates the tune will end after the strain or line is repeated.

A MAJOR SCALE
(Notice the key signature; the G is now ♯.)

Practice slowly. Gradually increase tempo and play as half, quarter, and eighth notes.

(After mastering the above scale, apply the models in Lesson 3 to each note above.)

Remember G is ♯. Refer to fingering chart for high B.

DOTTED EIGHTH NOTE EXERCISE

WEARING OF THE GREEN

fine (End)

D.C.
(Go to beginning)

Music from L. D. Walz Collection.

LESSON 6

THE TUNES in this lesson incorporate musical items included in the previous lessons. Pay close attention to time and key signatures, dotted eighth, quarter, and half notes, rests, and repeat signs.

"Yankee Doodle," a tune of somewhat uncertain origin composed sometime before 1767, is strongly associated with the Revolutionary War. Although a later version is slightly different and more melodic, the version popular during the years of the country's beginnings is printed here. A series of verses written by Edward Bangs about 1775 were used with the melody under the title "A Yankee's Return from Camp." The bottom line of "Yankee Doodle" includes harmony which allows the tune to be played as a duet or provides two-part harmony if executed by several fifers.

"The Cheat" was played in the early 1800s, often as accompaniment for a popular dance called the quadrille. Notice that the time signature is C (common time). Many pieces of music are written in common or 4/4 time. They may be played as marches by cutting the time in half. If this is done, the tunes would then be *alla breve*, or 2/2 time. The notation for 2/2 time is written ¢.

"Sweet Betsey from Pike" is an Americanization of an old English music hall song entitled "Vilikens and His Dinah." The tune, also known as "The Old Orange Flute," was popular in the United States soon after the California gold rush of 1849.

YANKEE DOODLE

Daniel Steele, *A New and Complete Preceptor for the German Flute* [1815].

THE CHEAT

tr

Steele, *New and Complete Preceptor for the German Flute* [1815].

SWEET BETSEY FROM PIKE

Mattson Arrangement.

LESSON 7

LINE 1 is an excellent exercise for developing embouchure and becoming familiar with the fingering in the high register. Play the lower scale and then the higher scale. Play each note for four slow beats, then play each note for two beats, then one beat. This should improve tone and technique.

Lines 2, 3, and 4 stress the use of sixteenth notes. A sixteenth note has two flags on the stem (♪) while an eighth note has only one (♪). Practice these exercises to improve fingering and tonguing.

"Old 1812 Quick Step" is a popular tune for fife and drum. It is composed of quarter, eighth, and sixteenth notes with an eighth rest. Observe the repeat signs. The origin of this tune has not been located, although it is known to have been in use before the Civil War and may, as its title suggests, have originated in the War of 1812.

Although fife music does not usually exceed high B, fingering for notes above high B is shown below to illustrate primary (P) and alternate (A) fingering for high C, C#, and D. The term "primary fingering" refers to the fingering considered most suitable to produce the note, while "alternate fingering," as the term implies, merely suggests another fingering method for sounding the same note.

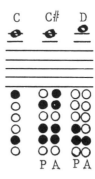

OCTAVE EXERCISE

SIXTEENTH NOTE EXERCISE

(Four sixteenth notes receive one beat.)

OLD 1812 QUICK STEP

The American Veteran Fifer, [1902].

LESSON 8

THIS LESSON is devoted to 6/8 (six-eight) time. Many tunes written for the fife are in 6/8 time; therefore careful study and attention to this rhythm is necessary. Six-eight time is a double rhythm subdivided into triplets. Slow music is played six beats to a measure. Fast music like marches is played two beats to a measure. Play the scale at the bottom of this page both ways (slow and fast).

Line 1 on the following page shows the rhythm figures commonly found in 6/8 time. Notice that the beat is depicted by numbers 1 through 6. First play the exercise six beats per measure. Then play the entire exercise again two beats per measure. Each group of eighth notes receives one beat.

Line 2 is a practice exercise for the rhythm figure of triplets. It can also be used to prac-tice triple tonguing, as can Line 1. Triple tonguing will be explained in Lesson 13.

"Silent Night" is played six beats to a measure. Notice the harmony written below the melody, thereby allowing the tune to be played as a duet. Of German origin, the song was first sung in Bavaria on Christmas Eve in 1818. It was written by Joseph Mohr, a Catholic priest, and became popular in the United States by the 1860s and 1870s.

"The Bonnie Blue Flag," a favorite with the Confederate soldiers of the Civil War, was second in popularity among them only to "Dixie." Originally this music was an old Irish air entitled "The Irish Jaunting Car." Words were added in 1861 by Irish comedian Henry McCarthy. The tune should be played in march time, two beats per measure.

SCALE
(in 6/8 time)

6/8 RHYTHM EXERCISE

```
1 2 3   4 5 6   12 3 45 6   123 456   123456   1 2 3 4 5 6   1 2 3   4 5 6   123 456   12 3  45 6
1 - -   2 - -   1-- 2 --   1-- 2--   1--2--   1 - - 2 - -   1 - -   2 - -   1-- 2--   1--   2--
```

SILENT NIGHT
(Duet)

Play six beats to a measure.

L. D. Walz Collection.

THE BONNIE BLUE FLAG

The American Veteran Fifer [1902].

LESSON 9

SIX-EIGHT RHYTHM is again stressed in this lesson. First play the tunes six beats to a measure and then repeat them at two beats to a measure.

"Pop Goes The Weasel" goes back at least to the period of the French and Indian War (1754-60) and possibly even further. It is thought to be a 17th-century children's song. In this tune the first and second endings of both strains are played. Play the first ending, repeat the entire strain, skip the first ending, and conclude the tune on the second ending.

"Tallewan" and "Carry Me Back to Old Virginny" are both pre-Civil War tunes. This version of the latter is much earlier than the now better-known James A. Bland song. First called "De Floating Scow of Virginia," it was written by Charles T. White, a well-known minstrel of the period, in 1847.

Notice that these tunes are written in the key of G. (Play the C natural.)

POP GOES THE WEASEL

L. D. Walz Collection.

33

CARRY ME BACK TO OLD VIRGINNY

The American Veteran Fifer [1902].

TALLEWAN

The American Veteran Fifer [1902].

LESSON 10

ALL THE TUNES of this lesson are in 2/4 time. This lesson combines the musical rudiments of the previous lessons.

Although probably an old Irish tune, "The Girl I Left Behind Me" became a popular British marching song under the title "Brighton Camp." In the years before the American revolution, it was often played when a British naval vessel set sail or an army unit left for service abroad. "The Girl I Left Behind Me" was adopted by the Americans and has become a traditional army song especially associated with the Seventh Infantry. It was also a favorite with the troops at Fort Snelling in the 19th century. Even today it is played at the United States Military Academy at West Point as part of the medley for the cadets' final formation for graduation.

"On the Road to Boston," also known as "General Greene's March," was one of the principal marches of the Revolutionary War. It is said to have been played by the troops of General Nathaneal Greene while on their way to the siege of Boston.

"My Love She's But a Lassie Yet," also known as "Johnny O," is an old Scottish air which was played by early American fifers and drummers from the latter part of the 18th century on.

THE GIRL I LEFT BEHIND ME

L. D. Walz Collection.

ON THE ROAD TO BOSTON
(General Greene's March)

Steele, *New and Complete Preceptor for the German Flute* [1815].

MY LOVE SHE'S BUT A LASSIE YET

William Williams, *A New and Complete Preceptor for the Fife*, 1826.

LESSON 11

ALL TUNES in this lesson are in 4/4 time. They are included as an aid to the development of tone and endurance and for their historical significance. Practice slowly to become familiar with the music and then play it in the correct tempo.

In the second tune, "Blue Bells of Scotland," an accidental sharp is introduced. If a sharp, flat, or natural is placed before a note, it changes the key signature of the note only for the measure in which it appears. "Blue Bells of Scotland," a late 18th-century Scottish air, was published in the United States as early as 1800 and played extensively before 1816.

If these tunes are to be played in march tempo, the time value must be reduced by half of its original value. This is known as cut time or 2/2 time. The symbol for cut time is ₵.

"Chester" was one of the most popular patriotic songs of the Revolutionary War. It was written by William Billings of Boston, the first American composer to make music his entire profession, and published in 1778. In spite of the song's popularity, Billings died in poverty.

"Finnigin's Wake" was originally a vaudeville tune which reached the height of its popularity in the United States during the 1860s.

CHESTER

James Hulbert, *The Complete Fifer's Museum,* [1807].

BLUE BELLS OF SCOTLAND

Steele, *New and Complete Preceptor for the German Flute* [1815].

FINNIGIN'S WAKE

The American Veteran Fifer, [1902].

LESSON 12

FIFERS are frequently called upon to play the "Star-Spangled Banner," which was composed by Francis Scott Key during the War of 1812 and which officially became the country's national anthem in 1931. Notice the accidental G♯ in the third, eleventh, and twenty-third measures. In the third and fifth measures from the end of the song, there is a hold sign ⌒ over a note. This means that the note will be held longer than its normal value. The sign also means *fine*, or finish, which indicates the end of a musical passage.

Not so well known is "To Anacreon in Heaven" (see page 86), a British drinking song used by Francis Scott Key as the basic melody for the "Star-Spangled Banner." Some authorities claim that the tune was originally French before it became British. The United States Marine Fife and Drum Corps played the melody of "To Anacreon in Heaven" for ceremonies in Washington, D.C., as early as 1817.

"St. Patrick's Day in the Morning" was reportedly played by the pipers of an Irish brigade at the battle of Fontenoy on May 11, 1745, and published as early as 1748. The tune has been popular with American fifers since the latter part of the 18th century. Practice the music slowly to ensure that the rhythm figures are played correctly. "St. Patrick's Day in the Morning" is ideally suited to playing in a fast tempo, and lends itself to triple tonguing, which is discussed in Lesson 13.

STAR-SPANGLED BANNER

L. D. Walz Collection.

ST. PATRICK'S DAY IN THE MORNING

Steele, *New and Complete Preceptor for the German Flute* [1815].

LESSON 13

THE THREE TUNES in this lesson cover the normal range of the fife and will improve the fifer's technique. Practice each tune slowly and increase the speed until the desired tempo is obtained.

"Montezuma," "College Hornpipe," and the "Highland Laddie" or "White Cockade" are outstanding hornpipe tunes and have been favorites with fifers throughout the years. "Montezuma" was probably inspired by the Mexican War. "College Hornpipe" and "White Cockade" were used in America in the late 1700s. The title means literally a "bouquet" and has nothing to do with the military cockade. Robert Burns added words to this old tune under the title "Highland Laddie." For "College Hornpipe," see page 56.

DOUBLE AND TRIPLE TONGUING

A method for fife instruction would not be complete without covering the use of double and triple tonguing. It may be necessary on occasion to play tunes faster than one can single tongue. Therefore, the fifer should be able to double or triple tongue.

Double Tonguing: Develop the articulation Ta Ka, Ta Ka, Ta Ka, Ta Ka. The tip of the tongue strikes the top of the upper front teeth on the syllable Ta. On the second syllable Ka, the rear of the tongue touches the upper rear portion of the roof of the mouth. Double tonguing is used for even rhythm tunes and figurations. Models 1 through 5 in Lesson 3 are useful for the practice of double tonguing. Then try a few tunes like "The Girl I Left Behind Me" as well as those included in this lesson.

Triple Tonguing: Develop one of the two following articulations. Ta Ta Ka, Ta Ta Ka, Ta Ta Ka. This is favored by most players. The other articulation is Ta Ka Ta, Ka Ta Ka, Ta Ka Ta, Ka Ta Ka. Triple tonguing is articulated in the same manner as the syllables for double tonguing except triple tonguing is articulated as a triplet or a series of triplets. Triple tonguing is used on triple rhythm tunes. Apply this method to scales and exercises. Practice slowly for accuracy and then increase in speed. Try triple tonguing "St. Patrick's Day in the Morning," the "Irish Washerwoman," and "Garry

Owen," a rollicking Irish tune dating from 1800 that has been associated with the Seventh U.S. Cavalry since the 1860s. Use Model 5 in Lesson 3 for additional practice.

MONTEZUMA

The American Veteran Fifer [1902].

HIGHLAND LADDIE or THE WHITE COCKADE

B. and J. Carr, *Evening Amusement* [1796].

LESSON 14

THE TRILL

Many old compositions for the fife include trills to add flavor and character to a tune. Older pieces of music often refer to a trill as a "shake." A trill is produced by the rapid playing of two notes a tone or a half tone apart. They are played in a fast, even manner similar to the warbling of a bird.

The older method of executing a trill (pre-1860) is to first sound the note above that which is written and then play the written note. The later method is to first sound the written note and then go to the next higher unwritten note. While some trills are easier to play than others, practice helps overcome roughness of tone in the more difficult ones.

The abbreviation "Tr" placed above a note signifies that the note should be trilled for its entire time value. Notice in "The Cheat" on page 27 that the G in the 5th measure from the end is played as a trill.

The following intervals are considered by the authors as unsuitable for trilling: Beginning with the first line below the staff D-E♭; D♯-E♮; E♭-F♮; E♮-F♮; B♭-C♮; C♯-D♯; D♯-E♮; E♭-F♮; E♮-F♮; F♮-F♯; G♯-A♮; A♭-B♭; A♮-B♮; A♯-B♮; B♭-C♮; B♮-C♮; B♮-C♯; and high C-D. The trills included in this lesson are more suitable for the fife to execute. Notice the various intervals and the fingering combinations below the notes to be trilled.

FIFE TRILLS

SELECTED TUNES FOR THE FIFE

The tunes printed in this booklet are arranged more or less in alphabetical order by title. They represent traditional fife and drum music dating from the American colonial period to the end of the Civil War. Many had their origins in popular dances of the era -- quick steps, waltzes, and allemandes -- while others came from ballads of ethnic origin or marches associated with the Revolutionary War. Most of them were in use during the early years of the nineteenth century and were played at Fort Snelling.

The musical histories of much of this music are obscure or confused. In some instances the same tunes were known by different titles and spanned national boundaries. Attempts to identify composers and origins have engaged the diligent efforts of many scholars over the years, and are beyond the scope of this booklet. However, brief notes on the backgrounds of the tunes as well as the source of the music here printed are appended.

Regardless of origin or period, the selections are sprightly and enjoyable to play, and the fifer who attempts them will experience a delightful historical and musical adventure.

ALLEMANDE

An *allemande* is a dance figure in the quadrille in which the man turns his partner. It is also used in square and folk dancing.

Williams, *A New and Complete Preceptor for the Fife*, 1826.

ALL'S WELL -- DUET

From "The English Fleet in 1342," a comic opera produced in London in 1805 and printed in the United States about 1820.

Williams, *Complete Preceptor for the Fife*, 1826.

AMERICAN MARCH

Steele, *New and Complete Preceptor for the German Flute* [1815].

THE BALL

Versions of this music also appear in Longman and Broderip, 1785, and Holyoke, 1800.

Edward Murphey Manuscript, Library of Congress, 1790.

BALTIMORE

Variously referred to as a French march or a French quick step, this tune is printed in such early fife manuals as Joshua Cushing's *The Fifer's Companion* [1804] and it appears in the Edward Murphey manuscript in the Library of Congress dated 1790.

Hulbert, *The Complete Fifer's Museum* [1807].

BONAPARTE'S MARCH

Steele, *New and Complete Preceptor for the German Flute* [1815]. Williams, *Complete Preceptor for the Fife*, 1826, has a different melody for this march.

BONNY JEAN

Possibly of Scottish origin. Published in 1797 by John Aitken of Philadelphia in "The Scots Musical Museum."

Steele, *New and Complete Preceptor for the German Flute* [1815].

BOSTON MARCH

Samuel Holyoke, who collected and published this tune in 1800, was a versatile Massachusetts musician and one of the country's earliest composers. He lived from 1762 to 1820.

Holyoke, *The Instrumental Assistant*, 1800.

BOSTON QUICK STEP

Holyoke, *The Instrumental Assistant*, 1800.

BRITISH MUSE

This melody was published as early as 1786 in   Holyoke, *The Instrumental Assistant*, 1800.
New Haven, Connecticut.

CAPTAIN MACKINTOSH

Holyoke, *The Instrumental Assistant*, 1800.

CAPTAIN DECATUR'S HORNPIPE

Holyoke, *The Instrumental Assistant*, 1800.

COLLEGE HORNPIPE

B. and S. Carr, *Evening Amusement* [1796].

COME HASTE TO THE WEDDING

Joshua Cushing, *The Fifer's Companion* [1804].

DASHING WHITE SERGEANT

Composed about 1826 by Sir Henry Rowley Bishop   *The American Veteran Fifer* [1902].
with words by General John Burgoyne.

DIXIE

Daniel Emmett, a northerner, wrote "Dixie" as a minstrel song before the Civil War. When the war started, the South claimed it as their own. Thus it became the most popular song of the Confederacy. It was also a favorite of Abraham Lincoln who upon occasion requested Union bands to play "Dixie."

The American Veteran Fifer [1902].

FISHER'S HORNPIPE

An old melody, possibly of Irish origin.   Carr, *Evening Amusement* [1796].

FRENCH AIR

Holyoke, *The Instrumental Assistant*, 1800.

GARRY OWEN

"Garry Owen," an Irish favorite, is said to have
been first played in 1800 in a pantomime entitled "Harlequin Amulet." *The American Veteran Fifer* [1902].

GENERAL WAYNE'S MARCH

General Anthony Wayne, who had a brilliant rec-
ord in the Revolutionary War, was sent by Washington in 1792 to subdue the Indians and bring
peace to the Ohio Valley.

Holyoke, *The Instrumental Assistant*, 1800.

GIVE ME THE GIRL THAT'S RIPE FOR JOY

Steele, *New and Complete Preceptor for the German Flute* [1815].

GO TO THE DEVIL AND SHAKE YOURSELF

This tune was a popular jig printed in London in 1798 and surviving for the next century in this form, virtually without variations.

Cushing, *The Fifer's Companion* [1804].

GREEN JOKE

Steele, *New and Complete Preceptor for the German Flute* [1815].

HAIL COLUMBIA
(President's March)

This music was composed in 1789 in honor of Wash- Holyoke, *The Instrumental Assistant*, 1800.
ington's election to the presidency probably by
Philip Phile. Words, added in 1798 by Joseph
Hopkinson, son of Francis, the first native American composer, made the song an instant success.
It appears in most of the fife manuals published
between 1800 and 1826.

HAIL TO THE CHIEF

This music was first played as a salute to the president in 1845 when James K. Polk was in the White House. Although it was used as late as 1862 as a salute for a general, it was often played for President Abraham Lincoln and later became the official music associated with an appearance of the president of the United States.

The American Veteran Fifer [1902].

HAY MAKER

Hulbert, *The Complete Fifer's Museum*, 1807.

HELL ON THE WABASH

This tune also appears in Bruce and Emmett, *The Drummer's and Fifer's Guide* [1862], and in *The American Veteran Fifer* [1902].   L. D. Walz Manuscript Collection.

IRISH WASHERWOMAN

Sometimes attributed to an Irish piper named
Jackson who flourished about 1750.

Carr, *Evening Amusement*, 1796.

KINGDOM COMING

Henry C. Work, the composer of this music in
1861 or 1862, is well known as the author of
"Marching Through Georgia" and many other tunes.

L. D. Walz Manuscript Collection.

LA PROMENADE

Cushing, *The Fifer's Companion* [1804].

LASS GEN YE LO'E ME

Williams, *Complete Preceptor for the Fife*, 1826.

LIBERTY SONG

The words for a "song of American freedom" were written by John Dickinson in 1768 and set to an English tune entitled "Heart of Oak," composed in 1759 by William Boyce. The "Liberty Song" was soon adopted by the Sons of Liberty and became popular before the Revolutionary War.

"Mary Mathers Book," 1810, a manuscript in the Library of Congress.

MISS M'LEOD

An Irish tune known in print as early as 1779 and danced as a reel in New England.

Williams, *Complete Preceptor for the Fife*, 1826.

MISSISSIPPI QUICK STEP

Bruce and Emmett, *The Drummer's and Fifer's Guide* [1862].

MOLLY PUT THE KETTLE ON

Steele, *New and Complete Preceptor for the German Flute* [1815].

OH DEAR, WHAT CAN THE MATTER BE

This tune, published in Philadelphia at least as early as 1793, appears in fife manuals over the years until 1862.

Holyoke, *The Instrumental Assistant*, 1800.

OLD CONTINENTAL MARCH (Quick Step)

Edward Murphey Manuscript, Library of Congress,
1790.

OLD DAN TUCKER

Although he did not write the music, words were
supplied to a published version of this tune in
1843 by Daniel D. Emmett, a fifer and a famous
minstrel who also composed "Dixie."

The American Veteran Fifer, 1902.

PORTLAND FAIR or TRIP TO THE HEART

Robinson, *Massachusetts Collection of Martial Musick*, 1820.

QUICK MARCH

Holyoke, *The Instrumental Assistant*, 1800.

QUICK STEP NO. 1

Williams, *Complete Preceptor for the Fife*, 1826.

QUICK STEP NO. 2

Williams, *Complete Preceptor for the Fife*, 1826.

QUICK STEP NO. 4

Williams, *Complete Preceptor for the Fife*, 1826.

QUICK STEP 17TH REGIMENT

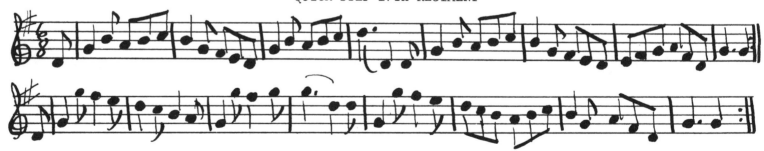

Edward Murphey Manuscript, Library of Congress, 1790.

ROSLIN CASTLE -- Death March

This melody was most often associated with funerals during the Revolutionary War period. The title refers to a Scottish castle located near Edinburgh. Versions appear in many other sources for the era.

Robinson, *Massachusetts Collection of Martial Musick*, 1820.

SERGEANT O'LEARY

L. D. Walz Manuscript Collection, circa 1860s.

SING SING POLLY

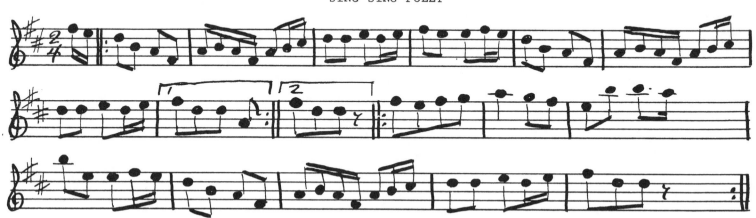

A song popular during the Civil War.   L. D. Walz Manuscript Collection, circa 1860s.

SOLDIER'S JOY

An old dance tune possibly of English origin.
This music also appears in Carr, 1796; Cushing,
1804; and Steele [1815].

Longman and Broderip, *Entire New and Compleat
Instructions for the Fife*, 1785.

SPANISH WAR SONG

Williams, *Complete Preceptor for the Fife*, 1826.

SURRY HORNPIPE

Williams, *Complete Preceptor for the Fife*, 1826.

THE AMERICAN EAGLE

Music bearing the same name but having a totally different melody appears in *The American Veteran Fifer* [1902].

Steele, *New and Complete Preceptor for the German Flute* [1815].

THE BLACK COCKADE

A version also appears in Cushing, 1804.   Holyoke, *The Instrumental Assistant*, 1800.

TO ANACREON IN HEAVEN

A British drinking song used by Francis Scott Key as the basic melody for the "Star-Spangled Banner." Published at least as early as the 1780s, the tune was also known as "Adams and Liberty."

Steele, *New and Complete Preceptor for the German Flute* [1815].

VILLAGE QUICK STEP

Composed by Dr. John C. Bartlett in 1843, this tune was popular during the Civil War years.

The American Veteran Fifer [1902].

WASHINGTON'S GRAND MARCH

or PRESIDENT'S NEW MARCH

This version, also known as "President's New March" appears to be slightly later in origin than that on p. 89, possibly having been composed for the president's inauguration in 1789.

Steele, *New and Complete Preceptor for the German Flute* [1815].

WASHINGTON'S MARCH

No less than eight marches under this title were uncovered by Oscar Sonneck's research, all seemingly composed during the last decades of the 18th century. This version is undoubtedly of Revolutionary War origin. It is sometimes entitled "Washington's March at the Battle of Trenton."

Carr, *Evening Amusement*, 1796.

WASHINGTON'S REEL

Holyoke, *The Instrumental Assistant*, 1800.

WHAT A BEAU YOUR GRANNY WAS

Carr, *Evening Amusement*, 1796.

WHEN FIRST I SAW &c

Holyoke, *The Instrumental Assistant*, 1800.

DUTIES IN CAMP AND GARRISON

THREE CHEERS

"Three Cheers" is said to have originated during the Crusades and has long been a part of military ceremonies. It was employed during the Revolutionary War as a co-ordinating signal or call, and it has been played when trooping the line and as part of a musical salute. The modern version has no trills and is known as "Sound Off."

The fingering shown for "Three Cheers" is a "false" fingering used by the Fort Snelling Fife and Drum Corps for ease in executing this musical phrase. False fingering is used to obtain a par-

ticular note or to execute a musical passage when it is not practicable to execute it by standard fingering methods. False fingering often produces notes that are not as true in pitch as those obtained by standard fingering. In the case of "Three Cheers," sound the lower note first and then the higher one.

The first version below is from Robinson, *Massachusetts Collection of Martial Musick*, 1820. The second version appears in Bruce and Emmett, *The Drummer's and Fifer's Guide* [1862].

1820 Version

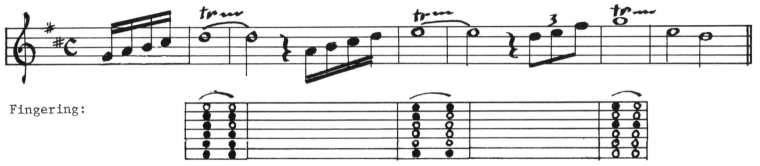

Fingering:

92

1862 Version

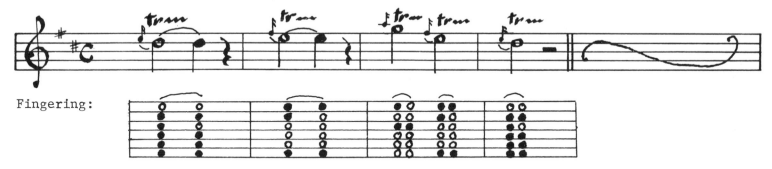

Fingering:

REVEILLE

Reveille sounded at daybreak as the signal for the men to rise. A long drawn-out ceremony, it included up to seven tunes, starting and ending with "Three Cheers." The Reveille given here was prescribed in General Winfield Scott's, *Infantry Tactics* (1835) and is basically the same as that played by the Continental Army.

The figures above the time signature for each tune indicate the rate at which the tune is to be played. For example, 140=♩ indicates that the tune is to be played at the rate of 140 quarter notes per minute.

Three Cheers

Three Camps or Points of War

First Camp

Slow Scotch

Drum Roll

The Austrian

Drum Roll

The Hessian

Drum Roll

Dutch

Drum Roll

Quick Scotch

Drum Roll

End of Reveille

The American Veteran Fifer, [1902].

PEAS UPON A TRENCHER

ROAST BEEF

"Peas Upon a Trencher" was the signal for break-fast and supper. "Roast Beef" was the call for dinner which was eaten about noon. It was also the signal to draw provisions. The U.S. Navy played this tune on board battleships with fifes and drums for evening officers' mess as late as 1892.

Robinson, *Massachusetts Collection of Martial Musick*, 1820.

TROOP

"The Troop" sounded to assemble the men for duty inspection, and guard mount. The first part of the music was also used as the Adjutant's Call. Note: "Three Cheers" are played prior to and after "The Troop."

G. Goulding, *New and Complete Instructions for the Fife*, ca. 1787. Other versions of this beat appear in Cushing, 1804, and Robinson, 1820.

TO ARMS

The drum normally plays a long roll with this call.

Robinson, *Massachusets Collection of Martial Musick*, 1820.

DRUMMER'S CALL

The Drummer's Call sounded to assemble the musicians.

Robinson, *Massachusetts Collection of Martial Musick*, 1820.

PIONEERS MARCH or FATIGUE CALL

This call was played for fatigue duty.

Bruce and Emmett, *The Drummer's and Fifer's Guide* [1862].

THE GENERAL

The General was the signal to strike the tents
and prepare for the march.

Robinson, *Massachusetts Collection of Martial
Musick*, 1820.

GENERAL'S SALUTE

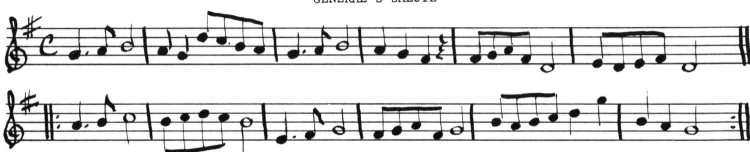

Another melody played as a general's salute may
be found in Hulbert, *The Complete Fifer's Museum*,
[1807]. "Hail to the Chief" is listed as a salute to a general in Bruce and Emmett, 1862.

Robinson, *Massachusetts Collection of Martial
Musick*, 1820.

DOUBLINGS

Doublings, originally used as a signal for increasing the troops, are played as an interlude strain between tunes. They were played by the Continental and later by the U.S. Army.

Longman and Broderip, *Entire New and Compleat Instructions for the Fife*, 1785. Robinson, *Massachusetts Collection of Martial Musick*, 1820.

DOUBLINGS WHEN COLORS ARE RECEIVED

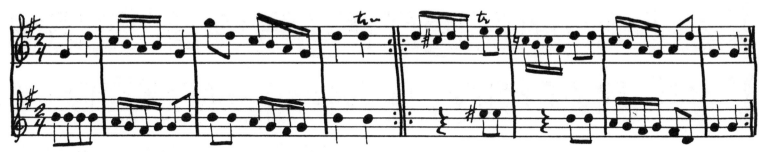

Played when performing as color escort, the in-   Cushing, *The Fifer's Companion* [1804].
stant the colors were brought out for a ceremony.

RETREAT TO BE PERFORMED AT SUNSET

Robinson, *Massachusetts Collection of Martial Musick*, 1820.

RETREAT

Versions of this tune also appear in Longman and Broderip, 1785; Goulding, ca. 1787; Cushing, 1804; Robinson, 1826; and Williams, 1826.

David Rutherford, *The Compleat Tutor for the Fife* [1756].

TATTOO

After Tattoo sounded in the evening, no soldier was "to be out of his tent or quarters," according to the 1836 regulations. The word "tattoo" came from the Dutch meaning "to shut," and was originally a signal for innkeepers to shut the taps on their kegs and close business for the day, during the Thirty Years War. Short and long tattoos were selected depending upon situations and weather conditions. The Long Tattoo was more appropriate for summer months.

Short Tattoo

The drums normally played a roll to accompany this call.

Robinson, *Massachusetts Collection of Martial Musick*, 1820

Long Tattoo

The Long Tattoo was a sequence of tunes some of which could be varied according to the occasion. "Three Cheers" begins the Long Tatoo, after which Doublings is played. Doublings is also used as an interlude strain between the various tunes and concludes the sequence after "Three Cheers" is again played.

First play "Three Cheers."

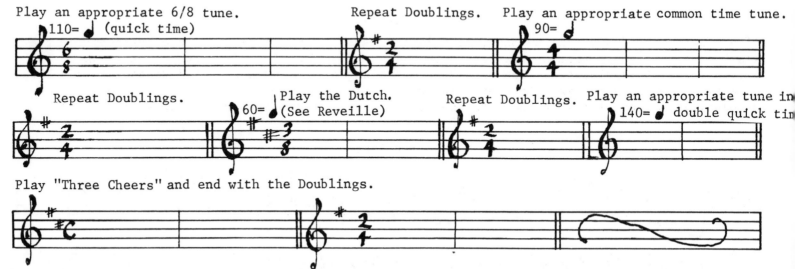

Sources from the Civil War period, proscribing a similar sequence of tunes for the Long Tattoo, suggest for the common time tune a national air such as "Hail to the Chief," and indicate that "Yankee Doodle" be played in place of the double-quick time tune.

Scott, *Infantry Tactics*, 1835.

BIBLIOGRAPHY

The American Veteran Fifer. Williamsburg, Va.: "Drummer's Assistant," [1902]. 80 p.

Ashworth, Charles S. *A New, Useful and Complete System of Drum Beating.* Washington, D.C.: 1812. Revised and supplemented by George P. Carroll, 1966. 40 p.

Baines, Anthony. *European and American Musical Instruments.* New York: Viking Press, 1966. 174 p.

Baltzer, Kenneth R. "American Instrumental Music of the Revolutionary War Period." University of Minnesota course paper, 1969. 171 p.

Bate, Philip. *The Flute: A Study of its History, Development and Construction.* London and New York: Ernest Benn Ltd. & W. W. Norton & Co., 1969. 268 p.

Bernard, Kenneth A. *Lincoln and the Music of the Civil War.* Caldwell, Idaho: Caxton Printers, Ltd., 1966. 333 p.

Bruce, George B. and Daniel D. Emmett. *The Drummer's and Fifer's Guide: or Self-Instructor.* New York: 1862. 96 p.

Camus, Raoul F. "The Military Band in the United States Army Prior to 1834." Ph.D. thesis, New York University, 1969. 535 p.

Carpenter, K. W. "A History of the United States Marine Band." 1970. 57 p.

Carr, B[enjamin] and J[oseph]. *Evening Amusement.* Philadelphia: B. and J. Carr. [1796]. 32 p. Copy in Library of Congress.

[Cushing, Joshua]. *The Fifer's Companion.* Salem, Mass.: Cushing and Appleton, [1804]. [81 p.]

Davis, Dennis C. "A History of Wind Instrument Manufacturing in the United States before 1900." University of Minnesota term paper, 1973. 25 p.

Dichter, Harry, and Elliott Shapiro. *Early American Sheet Music: Its Lure and Its Lore 1768-1889.* New York: R. R. Bowker Co., 1941. 287 p.

Dolph, Edward A. *"Sound Off!" Soldier Songs From the Revolution to World War II.* New York: Farrar & Rinehart Inc., 1942. 621 p.

Eliason, Robert E. "Early American Winds -- Instruments, Makers and Music." A paper read before the Am. Musicological Society, Dallas, 1972. 12 p. Copy in Kugler Museum of Musical Instruments.

Farmer, Henry George. *The Rise & Development of Military Music.* London: William Reeves, [n.d.]. 156 p.

Farrow, Edward S. *Farrow's Military Encyclopedia.* 3 vols. New York: published by author, 1885.

Ford, Ira W. *Traditional Music of America.* New York: E. P. Dutton and Company, Inc., 1940. 480 p.

Galpin, Francis W. *Old English Instruments of Music: Their History and Character.* 4th ed. rev. by Thurston Dart. London: Methuen & Co. Ltd., 1965. 254 p.

Galpin, Francis W. *A Textbook of European Musical Instruments: Their Origin, History, and Character.* New York: John de Graff Inc., 1937. 256 p.

Goulding, G. *New and Complete Instructions for the Fife.* London: published by author, [ca. 1787-99]. [32 p.]

Hixon, Donald L. *Music in Early America: A Bibliography of Music in Evans.* Metuchen, N.J., Scarecrow Press, Inc., 1970. 607 p.

Holyoke, Samuel. *The Instrumental Assistant.* vol.1. Exeter, N.H.; H. Ranlet, [1800]. 79 p.

Howard, John Tasker. *Our American Music: A Comprehensive History from 1620 to the Present.* New York: Thomas Y. Crowell Co., 1965. 944 p.

Hulbert, James. *The Complete Fifer's Museum.* Greenfield, Mass.: Ansel Phelps, [1807]. [24 p.].

Johnson, Helen K. *Familiar Songs With Historical Sketches of the Songs and their Authors.* New York: H. M. Caldwell Co., 1881. 660 p.

Kugler, William, Collection. Manuscript music for about 50 tunes and airs dating apparently from circa 1806. In Kugler Museum of Musical Instruments.

Linscott, Eloise H. ed. *Folk Songs of Old New England*. New York, Macmillan Co., 1939. 337 p.

Longman and Broderip. *Entire New and Compleat Instructions for the Fife*. London: Longman and Broderip, [1785]. 36 p.

Lord, Francis A. and Arthur Wise. *Bands and Drummer Boys of the Civil War*. New York and London: Thomas Yoseloff, 1966. 237 p.

The Martial Music of Camp Dupont. Philadelphia: George E. Blake, [1816]. 25 p.

Mathers, Mary, comp. "Mary Mathers Book," 1810. A manuscript collection of music in the Library of Congress. [158 p.]

Mattfeld, Julius. *Variety Music Cavalcade, 1620-1950: A Chronology of Vocal and Instrumental Music Popular in the United States*. New York: Prentice-Hall, 1952. 637 p.

Murphey, Edward, comp. Manuscript music collection of Edward Murphey, October 26, 1790. In Library of Congress. [40 p.]

Nathan, Hans. *Dan Emmett and the Rise of Early Negro Minstrelsy*. Norman: University of Oklahoma Press, 1962. 496 p.

Riling, Joseph R. *Baron Von Steuben and His Regulations*. Philadelphia: Ray Riling Arms Books Co., 1966.

Robinson, Alvan, Jr. *Massachusetts Collection of Martial Musick*. Durham, Me.: published by author, 1820. 71 p.

Rutherford, David. *The Compleat Tutor for the Fife*. London: published by author, [1756]. 21 p.

Sachs, Curt. *The History of Musical Instruments*. New York: W. W. Norton & Co., 1940. 505 p.

Scott, Winfield. *Infantry Tactics; or Rules for the Exercise and Manoeuvres of the United States Infantry*. vol. 1. New York: George Dearborn, 1835.

Sonneck, Oscar G. T. *A Bibliography of Early Secular American Music*. Revised and enlarged by William T. Upton. Washington, D.C.: Library of Congress, 1945. 616 p.

Steele, Daniel. *A New and Complete Preceptor for the German Flute*. Albany, N.Y.: published by author, [1815]. 34 p.

U. S. Marine Corps. *Manual for Drummer, Trumpeters, and Fifers*. Washington, D.C.: 1935

War Department: *Abstract of Infantry Tactics:*

Including Exercises and Manoeuvres of Light-Infantry and Riflemen for the Use of the Militia of the United States. Boston: Hilliard, Gray, Little and Wilkins, 1830. 138 p.

White, William C. *A History of Military Music in America.* Exposition Press, 1944.

Williams, William. *A New and Complete Preceptor for the Fife.* Utica, N.Y.: published by author, 1826. [28 p.]

Woodbury, William H. Snare Drum Music Played at Fort Snelling. Manuscript music in the Minnesota Historical Society.

INDEX OF TUNES